D1520047

Contents

What Is the Acropolis Museum?

The Acropolis Museum sits at the base of a mountain that has great significance to the people of Greece. At the top of the mountain sits what remains of the Acropolis. In ancient times, it served as the city center for the people of Athens. Over time, however, the buildings of the Acropolis began to deteriorate. Efforts were made to save what remained of the site, and a museum was built to house the site's **artifacts**. As the years passed, more artifacts were found, and the museum outgrew its space. The Acropolis Museum was built to accommodate the growing **collection** and the increasing number of visitors coming to see it.

The Acropolis Museum is located in a part of Athens called Makrygianni. The area is known for its rich history, which extends back to when Athens was controlled by the Roman Empire in the 200s AD.

The Acropolis Museum uses art, history, and **architecture** to tell the story of life in ancient Greece. Visitors to the museum can view the remains of buildings and everyday objects to gain a better understanding of how ancient Greeks lived and interacted with each other. They can also see sculptures of ancient gods and goddesses to learn about the spiritual beliefs of the ancient Greeks. The Acropolis Museum links the people of Greece to the history that has made the country what it is today. The museum is important to the world because it sheds light on a civilization that has fascinated people for centuries.

The Acropolis Museum's total area is **250,000 square feet** (23,000 square meters).

It cost about **$175 million** to build the museum.

Display space at the museum covers more than **150,000 square feet** (14,000 sq. m).

Since opening, the museum has had more than **6.5 million visitors**. At least **10,000 people** visit it every day.

History of the Acropolis Museum

The original Acropolis Museum was built in 1865 within yards (meters) of the Parthenon, the main temple at the site. As the collection grew, a second building was added to the museum. When this did not provide enough room, the original building was expanded. The museum continued to experience crowding issues, however. Ultimately, items were moved to museums in other countries. This loss of history resonated with the people of Greece. A movement began to build a museum that would properly house the artifacts still in Greece and allow the other artifacts to be brought back. Plans for this museum began to take shape in 1976, but were delayed. It was not until 2000 that the project began in earnest.

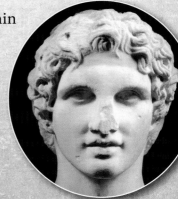

One of the sculptures originally transferred from the old Acropolis Museum to the new museum portrays Alexander the Great, the Macedonian leader who conquered Greece in the 300s BC.

1865 The **foundation** stone is laid for the first Acropolis Museum on December 30.

1976 In September, Konstantinos Karamanlis, the prime minister of Greece, proposes the building of a new museum at the Acropolis.

1850	1900	1950	1990

1888 Plans for a second building, called the Little Museum, are announced. It is torn down between 1946 and 1947, and the original museum is extended.

1976–1989 Three separate design competitions are held, but the project is delayed each time.

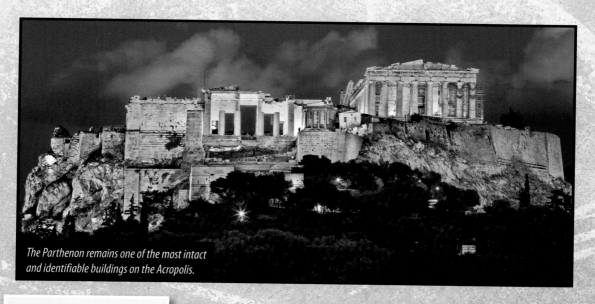
The Parthenon remains one of the most intact and identifiable buildings on the Acropolis.

2000 A new design competition for the museum is announced. Architects Bernard Tschumi and Michael Photiadis win the competition the following year.

2007 The museum is completed in September. Artifacts are moved into the building from September to December.

2009 The official public opening of the new Acropolis Museum takes place on June 20.

2000   **2003**   **2007**   **2010**

2002 The final design for the Acropolis Museum is completed and approved.

2003 The **groundbreaking** ceremony takes place in September, and construction on the new museum begins.

2008 Parts of the museum open to the public.

Key People

Many people played a role in getting the Acropolis Museum built. Members of government promoted the creation of the museum and provided the support needed to get the project started. Leading museum experts helped direct the work so that, when complete, the museum would showcase the collection and keep it in good condition. Architects developed models and designs to achieve these goals.

Konstantinos Karamanlis (1907–1998)

Konstantinos Karamanlis was born in the village of Próti in 1907. After finishing his basic schooling, Karamanlis attended the University of Athens, where he graduated with a law degree in 1932. Within three years, he had become a member of Greece's parliament. Karamanlis became the country's prime minister in 1955 and remained in the position until 1963. He was then re-elected in 1974 and led the country for another six years. In 1980, he became the country's president, holding that position from 1980 to 1985, and again from 1990 to 1995. Karamanlis was best known for helping improve the economy and connecting Greece with the European community.

In addition to proposing the creation of the museum, Konstantinos Karamanlis also selected the museum's location.

Dimitrios Pandermalis (1940–Present)

Dimitrios Pandermalis played an active role in the development of the Acropolis Museum. He sat on the selection committee for the museum's architects, and later served as president of the Organization for the Construction of the New Acropolis Museum. Graduating with a doctorate in **archaeology** in 1968, Pandermalis taught at various universities throughout Europe and the world, and went on numerous archaeological expeditions. After guiding the construction of the Acropolis Museum to completion, he was appointed its president.

Along with being the museum's president, Dimitrios Pandermalis is also a professor at the University of Thessaloniki.

Bernard Tschumi (1944–Present)

Bernard Tschumi was the lead architect and designer of the Acropolis Museum. Born in Switzerland, Tschumi graduated from the Swiss Federal Institute of Technology in 1969. He then embarked on a teaching career, lecturing at universities in England and the United States, before becoming dean of the Graduate School of Architecture at Columbia University. While teaching, he continued to act as the lead architect on many high-profile public and cultural projects, including the Acropolis Museum. Tschumi's work has earned him several awards. In 1996, he received France's *Grand Prix national d'architecture*. His design of the Acropolis Museum won a National Honor Award from the American Institute of Architects. Tschumi is currently a professor at Columbia University.

Bernard Tschumi is known internationally as one of the world's most innovative architects.

Michael Photiadis

Michael Photiadis was the associate architect of the Acropolis Museum. He attended Athens College before moving to the United States to continue his education. Photiadis received his Bachelor of Architecture from Oklahoma State University and his master's degree from the Massachusetts Institute of Technology. He played a key role in the design and set-up of the Acropolis Museum by providing a local point of view. His experience came from previous architectural work on office buildings, educational institutions, public buildings, and other museums.

Michael Photiadis has been a guest lecturer at universities throughout Europe and the United States.

The Acropolis Museum Today

Since its opening, the Acropolis Museum has been focused on providing visitors with a view to the past. The goal of the museum's organizers is to allow people to experience what life was like on the Acropolis in ancient Greece. These connections to the past are often achieved through technology. Digital images have been used to demonstrate the original carving processes used to create the structures that once stood on the Acropolis. **Virtual reality** displays and **three-dimensional (3D)** movies allow visitors to see re-creations of the site and its surroundings. People can also see how technology is being used to **conserve** and restore artifacts from the Acropolis. The museum supplements these learning opportunities with gallery talks, concerts, and other activities that allow visitors to interact with the **exhibits** and access more information about them.

The entrance to the museum points up to the Acropolis itself, making a clear connection between the building and the hilltop city.

Third Level

The Parthenon Gallery takes up the entire third floor of the museum. Here, visitors can view a video about the Parthenon and its sculptures before walking along a re-creation of the Parthenon's **frieze**.

Second Level

Visitors can take a break from viewing exhibits when they reach the second level. This floor features a restaurant, a gift shop, and the museum's multimedia center.

Ground Level

People enter the museum on the ground level. In addition to the ticket kiosk, this level features the museum's temporary exhibit space and virtual reality theater. The highlight of this level is a gallery that shows artifacts from the hillside of the Acropolis.

First Level

The first level is divided into two main parts. One gallery shows the early stages of the Acropolis' development. The other gallery showcases artifacts that came later in the site's history.

Touring the Acropolis Museum

A tour of the Acropolis Museum takes a specific path. People start their journey at the ground level and then tour half of the first level before continuing up to the third level. Their tour through the history of the Acropolis is completed on the other half of the first level. In this way, there is a distinct beginning and end to the story of the Acropolis.

Gallery of the Slopes of the Acropolis The centerpiece of the museum's ground level is the Gallery of the Slopes of the Acropolis. Visitors walk over its inclined, glass floors to see artifacts displayed below. Many of these objects were taken from **sanctuaries** and temples that had existed on the slopes of the Acropolis. The buildings had been used for religious gatherings as well as for theatrical performances.

Many of the artifacts on display in the Gallery of the Slopes of the Acropolis were used in the daily lives of the ancient Greeks.

Sculptures in the Archaic Gallery are positioned so they can be viewed from all sides. This allows visitors a three-dimensional view of the works.

Archaic Gallery The Archaic Gallery takes visitors on a journey through the early years of the Acropolis. Artifacts from the 7th century BC until the end of the **Greco-Persian Wars** in 479 BC are positioned so visitors can see them from all sides, in a naturally lit setting. This period of time was known for growth in Greek businesses and advances in art.

Parthenon Gallery This gallery features artifacts arranged to tell a story about the politics, ceremonies, battles, and rituals of ancient Greece. Viewing the artifacts while looking out windows to the remains of the actual Parthenon allows visitors to imagine the building as it once was.

Visitors view artifacts from the Parthenon by walking around the outside walls of the gallery, much like they would have walked around the building itself.

5th Century BC to 5th Century AD Gallery This gallery shows the history of the Acropolis in its later years. Visitors can view sculptures of noted leaders and **philosophers**. They can also see the remains of some of the key structures built on the Acropolis during this period.

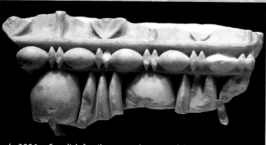

In 2006, a Swedish family returned a piece of the Erechtheion, one of the many temples of the Acropolis, to Greece. It is now on display on the museum's first level.

The Acropolis Museum has **more than 3,000** artifacts in its collection.

The museum stands **980 feet** (300 m) southeast of the Parthenon.

The artifacts in the Gallery of the Slopes of the Acropolis date from **3000 BC** to the **6th century AD**.

With 348 glass panels on its outer walls, the museum's top floor provides a **360 degree** view of Athens.

The museum sits aboveground on **43 concrete pillars**. Visitors can see the remains of a town underneath.

The new Acropolis Museum is almost **10x** larger than the original museum.

The **Parthenon frieze** contains more than **200** sculptures of animals.

It took about **15 years** to build the Parthenon.

The frieze is **524 feet** (160 m) long.

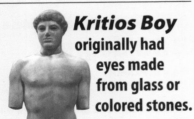

Kritios Boy originally had eyes made from glass or colored stones.

3 cranes were used to transfer more than **300 sculptures** from the old museum to the new museum.

The Acropolis Museum has **5 of the 6** Caryatids. The sixth sculpture is on display in the British Museum in London, England.

Treasures of the Acropolis Museum

Developing and maintaining a collection based on **antiquities** has many challenges. Artifacts can be damaged or be missing parts. Sometimes, this is due to their age and the conditions they have experienced over the years. In other cases, pieces may have been taken or sent to museums in other countries, where they became part of their collections. For all of these reasons, the Acropolis Museum has had to be innovative in the way it puts together its exhibits. While some pieces are on display in their damaged state, others are a combination of original and replacement pieces.

Some pieces are damaged to a point where they cannot be re-created. Still, the detail of what remains of the work allows visitors to gain a better understanding of who the ancient Greeks were and what was important to them.

The frieze is a continuous series of 115 blocks carved on a flat surface.

Parthenon Frieze The Parthenon frieze is the Acropolis Museum's main attraction. A combination of original sculptures and **plaster** re-creations, the frieze shows the full story of the Great Panathenaia, a festival held to honor the goddess Athena. Men and women are pictured carrying gifts to the statue of the goddess.

Caryatids These six statues of maidens once formed the columns that supported the south porch of the Erechtheion. Underneath the porch was the grave of King Kekrops of Athens. For this reason, it is believed that the Caryatids paid tribute to the dead.

Each Caryatid stands more than 7.5 feet (2.3 m) tall. No two Caryatids are the same.

Kritios Boy Created in about 480 BC, *Kritios Boy* is a marble sculpture that measures approximately 46 inches (1.17 m) in height. The figure stands on one leg with the other leg bent to suggest motion. The statue is believed to represent an athlete.

Kritios Boy *was found in two pieces. The torso was found in 1865. The head was found 23 years later.*

Pediments The Parthenon's **pediments** were located on each end of the building. They were the last pieces of the building to be sculpted. The scenes on the pediments show two important events in Greek mythology. The east pediment shows the birth of Athena. The west pediment portrays a battle for the land of Attica.

The museum features re-creations of the Parthenon's pediments to allow visitors to see the stories told on the original building.

Collection Conservation

A critical role of any museum is to conserve its collection. This ensures that the objects and works of art within the collection will be preserved for future generations so that they, too, can connect with the past. Conservators are the people directly involved with maintaining the condition of each artifact or piece of art. At the Acropolis Museum, conservators are tasked with the cleaning, repair, storage, and shipping of ancient sculptures and other works. They must know the proper techniques to use in every step of the conservation process.

Laser Technology After standing on the Acropolis for centuries, the sculptures have acquired layers of dirt, grime, and pollution. Before putting them on display, the works go through a thorough cleaning process using laser technology. Lasers beam rays of **infrared** and **ultraviolet radiation** over the sculptures in small sections, burning the layers of grime off slowly to reveal the original color of each individual work.

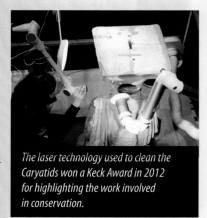

The laser technology used to clean the Caryatids won a Keck Award in 2012 for highlighting the work involved in conservation.

Saving Surfaces Exposure to the elements has damaged the surfaces of many of the Acropolis' structures. Marble has become pitted, and pieces have broken off. Some pieces have experienced sugaring. This is deterioration due to salt accumulation and excessive moisture. Conservators work to **consolidate** the surface. This means reattaching missing pieces and filling in pits. They use glues and chemical sprays to do this work.

Restoration work requires great focus and attention to detail.

Conservators took time to clean the remnants of the Parthenon's frieze before moving them from the old Acropolis Museum to the new museum.

Providing Support When the sculptures were removed from the Acropolis, many of them were taken off their original bases. Upon arrival at the museum, they were affixed to new bases that were specially designed to allow for better mobility. The statues could now be safely taken from their display space for conservation work. The bases were made out of marble similar to the museum floor so that they would not distract visitors from the statues themselves.

Besides providing ease of mobility, the standard look of the new bases helps to focus the viewer's attention on the works themselves.

Filling in the Gaps Some of the damage to structures has gone beyond the surface, resulting in cracks and holes in the marble. Before closing up these areas, conservators take steps to clean them so that they will not deteriorate further. Some gaps are cleaned by having air blown into them to remove dust and dirt. Other areas are wiped clean using **deionized** water and hydrogen peroxide. Once clean, the crack or hole is then filled with a cement-based mixture.

Conservators use a variety of small tools to repair cracked sculptures.

The Acropolis Museum in the World

One of the main goals of a museum is to educate the public about its collections and show their relevance in the world today. The Acropolis Museum has several programs designed to engage people in discussions about history, the arts, and mythology. Some of these programs are for visitors to the museum. Others reach out to people in faraway places.

Gallery Talks Museum archaeologists and other experts give gallery talks to visitors to provide more information about the exhibits. These talks are held at specific times throughout the day and take place in different locations. Talks are often tied in to specific galleries. In the Parthenon Gallery, visitors can attend a discussion about the role the Parthenon plays in the cultural history of the world. Following the talks, the speaker is available to answer questions and add more insight into the topic.

Gallery talks at the Acropolis Museum are provided in English, French, and Greek.

Backpacking in the Museum

The museum has created a series of kits for families to use as they tour the museum. Each kit comes in a bag similar to a backpack. Inside the bag are booklets and activities related to specific exhibits or themes. Families may find themselves going on a treasure hunt in the museum or creating their own works of art. The kits allow families to interact with the exhibits in a more personal way.

The museum's backpacks allow families to experience the exhibits together and to learn from each other.

Museum Friends In 2008, a group of Americans banded together to form an organization called American Friends of the New Acropolis Museum. The goal of the organization is to promote the museum in the United States and around the world, with the hope that people will visit the museum and support it financially. The group provides information to people wanting to learn more about the work of the museum. It also supports exchange study programs between American and Greek experts.

Michael Dukakis, a presidential candidate for the Democratic Party in 1988, is the Honorary Chair of the American Friends of the New Acropolis Museum organization.

Online Applications Staff at the Acropolis Museum have created several online applications for people who cannot experience the museum firsthand. Some of the apps follow the format of the backpacks, allowing people to participate in games and activities similar to those found in the bags. Others are more adult-oriented, providing online visitors with background information about some of the sculptures and artifacts found inside the museum.

Visitors to the museum's website can use an app to take a virtual tour of the galleries.

Looking to the Future

The British Museum has approximately half of the original sculptures from the Parthenon.

One of the Acropolis Museum's key goals for the future is to acquire as many of the Acropolis's original artifacts as possible. This means campaigning for the return of pieces that are now in museums outside of Greece. The best-known museum to hold Acropolis sculptures is the British Museum. The Parthenon sculptures were taken to England in the early 1800s and are now an important part of the British Museum's collection. The museum has declined requests from Greece to return the sculptures. Representatives for both sides continue to discuss the issue.

In the meantime, the Acropolis Museum continues to look for new ways to educate people about life in ancient Greece. In 2014, the museum announced that it will be opening a new exhibit that will showcase how everyday people lived in the past. Located outside of the main building, it will rely on objects from an archaeological dig taking place underneath the museum.

The city underneath the museum has fascinated visitors ever since it was discovered. The new exhibit will help explain how the city was organized and showcase some of the artifacts archaeologists have found on the site.

Activity

The Acropolis Museum's backpack program gives families a chance to learn about the museum's exhibits in a creative and hands-on way. The bags have books, games, models, and copies of ancient items that help bring the exhibits and artifacts to life. By using the materials in the backpacks, families have the opportunity to gain valuable insight into the meaning behind some of the structures on the Acropolis and the role they played in the lives of ancient Greeks.

Imagine you work as an educator at the Acropolis Museum. Create at least two materials for a backpack that will help families learn about a specific part of the museum.

Follow the steps below to put together your backpack.

1. Go to the Acropolis Museum's website, and select a section of the museum that you think needs a backpack.

2. List the specific artifacts or sculptures in this area.

3. Using your library or the internet, research these pieces to determine why they were important to the ancient Greeks.

4. From your research, develop a game that would teach others about these items. This could be a matching game or a quiz game.

5. Develop an activity that would allow the family to create their own version of one of the artifacts. This could involve drawing, painting, or sculpting with playdough.

6. Design a pamphlet about the contents of your backpack. Be sure to explain how each of the materials should be used.

Acropolis Museum Quiz

1 When did the new Acropolis Museum officially open?

2 Where is the Acropolis Museum located?

3 Who designed the Acropolis Museum?

4 Which gallery takes up the entire third floor of the museum?

5 How many Caryatids are on display at the Acropolis Museum?

ANSWERS:

1. 2009 2. At the base of the Acropolis in Athens, Greece
3. Bernard Tschumi and Michael Photiadis 4. Parthenon
Gallery 5. Five

Key Words

antiquities: objects from ancient times

archaeology: the study of the human past using material remains

architecture: the design of buildings and other structures

artifacts: objects that were made by people in the past

collection: works of art or other items collected for exhibit and study in a museum, and kept as part of its holdings

conserve: to protect an object from deterioration

consolidate: to make something physically stronger

deionized: removed charged atoms from a liquid

exhibits: displays of objects or artwork within a theme

foundation: a structure that supports a building from underneath

frieze: a decorative band found above a doorway or along a ceiling

Greco-Persian Wars: a series of wars that took place between Persia and Greece from 492 to 442 BC

groundbreaking: the breaking of soil at the start of a construction project

infrared: energy at wavelengths longer than those of visible light

pediments: triangular structures that form part of the front of a building

philosophers: people who study ideas about truth and the meaning of life

plaster: a soft mixture of lime, water, and sand or cement

radiation: the process of sending energy in the form of light, heat, or x-rays

sanctuaries: religious or holy places

three-dimensional (3D): having an illusion of depth behind a flat surface

ultraviolet: energy at wavelengths shorter than those of visible light

virtual reality: a realistic simulation of an environment

Index

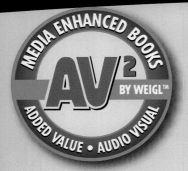

Log on to www.av2books.com

AV² by Weigl brings you media enhanced books that support active learning. Go to www.av2books.com, and enter the special code found on page 2 of this book. You will gain access to enriched and enhanced content that supplements and complements this book. Content includes video, audio, weblinks, quizzes, a slide show, and activities.

AV² Online Navigation

Book Pages
AV² pages directly correspond to pages in the book.

Audio
Listen to section the book read al

Video
Watch informati video clips.

Embedded Weblin
Gain additional informatio for research.

Try This!
Complete activities and hands-on experiments.

Key Words
Study vocabulary, and complete a matching word activity.

Quizzes
Test your knowledge.

Slide Show
View images and captions, and prepare a presentation.

AV² was built to bridge the gap between print and digital. We encourage you to tell us what you like and what you want to see in the future.

Sign up to be an AV² Ambassador at www.av2books.com/ambassador.

Due to the dynamic nature of the Internet, some of the URLs and activities provided as part of AV² by Weigl may have changed or ceased to exist. AV² by Weigl accepts no responsibility for any such changes. All media enhanced books are regularly monitored to update addresses and sites in a timely manner. Contact AV² by Weigl at 1-866-649-3445 or av2books@weigl.com with any questions, comments, or feedback.